2/04

THE LIBRARY OF
AMERICAN
LIVES AND TIMES™

GEORGE ARMSTRONG CUSTER

The Indian Wars and the Battle of the Little Bighorn

Paul Christopher Anderson

Clemson University

The Rosen Publishing Group's

PowerPlus Books™
New York

For the little boy Mack, who stood against long odds
—and won

Published in 2004 by The Rosen Publishing Group, Inc.
29 East 21st Street, New York, NY 10010

First Edition

Editor's Note: All quotations have been reproduced as they appeared in the letters and diaries from which they were borrowed. No correction was made to the inconsistent spelling that was common in that time period.

Library of Congress Cataloging-in-Publication Data

Anderson, Paul Christopher.
George Armstrong Custer : the Indian Wars and the Battle of the Little Bighorn / Paul Christopher Anderson.—1st ed.
    v. cm.—(The library of American lives and times)
Includes bibliographical references and index.
Contents: Remembering Custer—The boy from New Rumley—"Fanny"—Autie Custer's first war—Wolverine in blue—A warrior without a war—Frustrated frontiersman—A life on the Plains—To the Little Bighorn and beyond—Heroes and history.
  ISBN 0-8239-6631-3
1. Custer, George Armstrong, 1839–1876—Juvenile literature. 2. Little Bighorn, Battle of the, Mont., 1876—Juvenile literature. 3. Indians of North America—Wars—Juvenile literature. 4. Generals—United States—Biography—Juvenile literature. 5. United States. Army. Cavalry, 7th—Biography—Juvenile literature. [1. Custer, George Armstrong, 1839–1876. 2. Little Bighorn, Battle of the, Mont., 1876. 3. Indians of North America—Wars. 4. Generals.] I. Title. II. Series.
  E83.876.C983A53 2004
  973.8'2'092—dc21

                                                    2002153404

Manufactured in the United States of America

CONTENTS

1. Remembering Custer

The soldiers' bodies lay under the burning Montana sun. On June 25, 1876, George Armstrong Custer was dead, along with more than two hundred American soldiers who had followed him into battle. Many of the men, including Custer, had been stripped of their clothing. Sioux Indians had killed these men at the Battle of the Little Bighorn.

According to a tale told by a Cheyenne named Kate Bighead, which, as with so many stories told about Custer, may or may not be true, two Cheyenne women approached Custer's body after the battle. The women pierced Custer's eardrums with a sewing awl. They did this, Kate said, to improve his hearing. Custer had not listened to the Indians. Years before, the Indians had warned Custer that if he did not keep peace with them he would be killed. No one who later came upon the soldiers' bodies checked Custer's eardrums. Had they done

Opposite: Mathew Brady's studio took this portrait of George Armstrong Custer around 1864. The starred epaulets, or shoulder straps, on Custer's uniform signify his rank as a major general. During a battle, soldiers can quickly identify the commander by badges such as these.

so, we might know for certain whether Kate Bighead's story is true.

As it was, the undisputed truth was shocking enough. On the afternoon of June 25, George Armstrong Custer and the soldiers he commanded, the Seventh U.S. Cavalry, attacked a large camp of Sioux along the banks of the Little Bighorn River in Montana. Although the Sioux outnumbered the American soldiers by at least three to one, Custer chose to divide his men. The Seventh Cavalry was overwhelmed. The Sioux forced one group of Custer's soldiers into a panicked retreat. These men barely managed to escape. The other soldiers, the group that remained with Custer, were all killed.

For many white Americans, the Battle of the Little Bighorn was a national tragedy. The electronic telegraph system, a relatively new invention, shuttled lurid details of the battle to newspapers across the country. The nation's papers scrambled for additional details and

printed their stories under bold black headlines. The battle provoked all sorts of opinions and emotions. The most widespread feelings seemed to be a wish for revenge against the Sioux and deep admiration for Custer and his men. Custer's Last Stand, as many people called the battle, quickly became a legend. The battle's leader, who was already a national hero, became legendary.

More than a century after the event, people still talk and write about George Armstrong Custer. By one estimate, more books have been written about Custer than about any other American except Abraham Lincoln.

On the surface, Custer's compelling presence in American history seems unlikely. Other military leaders have died on the battlefield, and many of these leaders were better soldiers. There were other military leaders who were equally brave, and whose commands were devastated in other, more important battles.

So why does Custer live on in the American imagination? Partly because he was already a symbol and a mythic figure to Americans, even as he lived. Heroes have always represented the values of the culture that created them. America in Custer's time was a young, aggressive, and confident nation. Americans valued opportunity, challenge, and success. They prided themselves on the virtues of their government and the natural beauty of their country. More important, when they thought of opportunity, challenge, success, and natural beauty, many of them thought specifically about the American West.

Custer embodied all these ideals. He was bold, independent, and fearless, and he radiated physical vitality and charisma. In person, he was handsome. In fact, Custer's long, curly yellow hair achieved fame all by itself. Many of the nation's other celebrated figures, including political leaders and other soldiers, seemed boring and drab when compared to him. Custer went from being the youngest Civil War general to being the most renowned frontiersman of the West. He represented both the glory of the nation's past and the strength of its future.

Most of all, it seemed that no matter how great the odds, Custer could never be beaten. Fortune smiled on

---

Previous spread: The Seventh Calvary was photographed near Fort Hays, Kansas, in 1869. Custer rigorously drilled the cavalry in maneuvers, and the men who served under him had no choice but to obey his orders. Corporal Jacob Horner wrote, "When he got a notion, we had to go."

The Little Bighorn River originates in the Bighorn Mountains in Wyoming, flows north down the Little Bighorn Valley, and empties into the Bighorn River near present-day Hardin, Montana. The Crow named the area south of the Little Bighorn battlefield Greasy Grass. Crow legend states that when warriors passed through the area to water their ponies at the Little Bighorn River, the early morning dew on the foxtail barley left greaselike marks on the horses' chests. The Sioux also came to call the area Greasy Grass. Hence, the Battle of the Little Bighorn is known among Native Americans as the Battle of the Greasy Grass.

him, just as Americans believed that fortune smiled on their nation. He had what admirers called Custer's Luck.

The other part of Custer's continuing allure has to do with how we recall the past. Understanding this helps us to comprehend how people approach history. Some people continue to remember Custer because, to

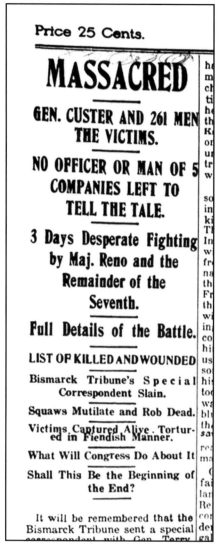

Price 25 Cents.

MASSACRED

GEN. CUSTER AND 261 MEN THE VICTIMS.

NO OFFICER OR MAN OF 5 COMPANIES LEFT TO TELL THE TALE.

3 Days Desperate Fighting by Maj. Reno and the Remainder of the Seventh.

Full Details of the Battle.

LIST OF KILLED AND WOUNDED

Bismarck Tribune's S p e c i a l Correspondent Slain.

Squaws Mutilate and Rob Dead.

Victims Captured Alive. Tortured in Fiendish Manner.

What Will Congress Do About It

Shall This Be the Beginning of the End?

It will be remembered that the Bismarck Tribune sent a special

This clipping was taken from the July 6, 1876, *Bismarck Tribune*. National newspapers covered the story for months. Many journalists were prejudiced against Native Americans, and this headline makes no mention of Native American casualties.

them, he lived in a more exciting, adventurous time. Our modern world, with its fast-food restaurants, its computers, its traffic, and its brisk pace, seems hectic, gritty, and crowded when compared to life on the nineteenth-century frontier.

Perhaps the most important point is that how history is remembered often reflects the passions and concerns of the present. To the people who lived in his time, as well as for many years after, Custer was a hero. Only later did Americans begin to feel guilty about what the nation had done to the Native Americans. Indians also began to demand that their experiences be remembered. In the name of progress, Americans had forced

Indian tribes from their lands. Americans had lied to the Indians, had broken promises to them, and had used the U.S. military to attack and defeat them. This, too, was part of Custer's story.

George Armstrong Custer represents both American achievement and American ruthlessness. He continues to live in our imagination because American history, like the histories of other peoples, is the story of who we are. When Americans today ask who they are, they are asking what they have done right and what they have done wrong. Custer can be used to answer both questions.

There may be one last twist in the Custer legend. In the tale that ended at the Little Bighorn, Custer came to represent the underdog. He became symbolic of devotion in the face of impossible odds. After all, he was desperately outnumbered at the battle. Americans still like to think of themselves as underdogs, and Custer's Last Stand echoes their belief in holding on despite the odds. However, the historical reality was quite different. In the struggle to claim the West, Americans were not the underdogs. They had the power to conquer. Americans were so strong that they didn't have to listen to their opponents, as Kate Bighead's story shows. The odds, indeed, were stacked against the Indians.

2. The Boy from New Rumley

George Armstrong Custer was born in New Rumley, Ohio, on December 5, 1839. He went by the name Autie. When he was learning to talk, he couldn't pronounce Armstrong. The word came out of his mouth as Autie, so that's what his parents, his siblings, and his friends called him.

Autie's parents, Emanuel and Maria Ward Kirkpatrick Custer, were a fairly typical American family, neither rich nor poor. Emanuel was a blacksmith who earned his living by making and repairing metal goods, such as horseshoes and farm tools, for his neighbors. Maria cared for the Custer children and tried her best to keep up with all the chores of running a busy, crowded household.

Both Emanuel and Maria Custer had been married before. Each had lost a spouse to an early death. Nineteenth-century America was safer and healthier than eighteenth-century America, but it was still not unusual for adults to die young. Accidents and untreatable illnesses were common. When Emanuel married Maria in 1836, he brought two sons with him, and Maria

This is a photograph of Custer's birthplace in New Rumley in eastern Ohio. The Custer home was situated high on a hilltop. The grade of the hill was so steep that horses required a rest midway before continuing to pull heavy carriages or wagons up the slope.

brought a son and a daughter with her. The Custer household became even more cramped when Emanuel and Maria began having children together. Autie was their first child to survive infancy. Four more children, three sons and a daughter, followed. Autie was remarkably close to his older stepsister, Lydia Ann, whom he called Ann, and closer still to his younger brothers Thomas and Boston, whom he called Tom and Bos.

By the time of Emanuel's marriage to Maria, the Custer family was well established in New Rumley. Ohio, however, was still a young state. Although it had been admitted to the Union in 1803, in places it still resembled

Although Emanuel Custer struggled to support his large family, Autie later told his father that he "never wanted for anything . . . ."

a frontier. Because towns were new and still being settled, the people who lived in them could sometimes be rowdy and brash. Emanuel was known for loudly voicing his opinions and playing practical jokes, qualities that would soon emerge in his son Autie. In politics, Emanuel was also known for his support of the Democratic Party, a loyalty that Autie would maintain as he grew up. The Democrats billed themselves as the party of the common people. They considered their opponents, the Whigs, to be a party that helped only the wealthy. Emanuel's neighbors thought enough of him to elect him to four consecutive terms as justice of the peace.

Emanuel's other great passion was the militia. In the nineteenth century, men from local communities often joined voluntary military groups. Citizens did this partly to protect their communities, and partly for the companionship. Militia day was both a day for training and a fun social event. When the militia gathered, the men would drill

Maria Custer, Autie's loving mother, believed that it was "sweet to toil for those we love."

Politics was a significant part of frontier life in the first part of the nineteenth century, especially for white men, who were the only people allowed to vote. A few years before Autie was born, Americans began to organize into two main political parties, the Democrats and the Whigs.

The first leader of the Democrats was Andrew Jackson, who was elected president in 1828. Democrats believed in restricting the powers and activities of the federal government. Many Democrats had small farms, or small businesses, or were mechanics or laborers. They suspected that a large government would grant privileges and bene-fits to the wealthy and would unfairly damage their own economic opportunities. Democrats also tended to favor westward expansion.

Whigs, on the other hand, believed that the federal government ought to play a strong, active role in building the nation's economy. Whigs tended to be people such as lawyers, bankers, southern plantation owners, and wealthy industrialists. Eventually, the Republican Party would replace the Whigs.

together in front of the community. When they finished, they would mingle, talk, and laugh with their neighbors. Emanuel was a member of the militia company called the New Rumley Guards.

Emanuel, who called Autie "my yellow-haired laddie," brought his son to many militia days. The boy was fascinated with the drills, the parades, and the shiny buttons on the uniforms. He loved to watch the militia leaders ride on horseback, for Autie loved horses above all. Often, dressed in his own homemade uniform, Autie brought along his toy gun and wooden sword. Sometimes, to Autie's inexpressible joy, the Guards would allow the boy to drill with them.

The military would always be special to Autie Custer because the military was where he could best be himself. Autie needed to be around people; he needed to fit in with a group. He also needed to be in front of people, to lead them and occasionally to perform for them. Indeed, Autie was a rambunctious child, and his parents had a hard time disciplining him. He was much fonder of wrestling with his brothers and playing jokes on his friends than he was of school. Autie was a smart boy, but his schoolwork bored him. When he was almost ten, Emanuel and Maria hired out Autie to a furniture maker, hoping the labor would discipline him. Autie hated the work.

Finally, in 1852, his parents decided to send him away to school in Monroe, Michigan, where his stepsister lived.

They knew how much Autie admired his stepsister. Ann was fourteen years older than Autie, and she treated her brother like a son and a best friend. She lived in Monroe with her husband, David Reed, a businessman whom she had married in 1846. Whether Autie did any better on his schoolwork in Monroe is debatable. He certainly continued his pranks. One day in church, he and his friends flicked metal pellets at the rest of the congregation, pelting them as they prayed. "We knew who was the promoter of such schemes," the minister later said, "for George was easily their leader."

Autie flourished in Ann's household and came to think of Monroe as his hometown. When he returned to New Rumley in 1855, he did so with disappointment.

By the time of Autie's sixteenth birthday, he had not come to a decision about what to do with his life. If his experience as a furniture maker was any indication, manual labor would bore him. He tried teaching for a few months in 1855 and 1856, but he was no more enthusiastic about attending school as a teacher than he had been as a student. He might have chosen to be a farmer. Most Americans of his time, after all, were farmers.

There was still another possibility. Although Autie didn't have the homemade uniform or the wooden sword anymore, he thought he could become a soldier.

3. School and Skins

George Armstrong Custer believed that the events in his life always worked to his benefit. His continual good fortune would later be known as Custer's Luck. The first of many good strokes of fortune occurred in 1856, when Autie decided that he would apply to the U.S. Military Academy in West Point, New York.

Autie decided on West Point because he recalled the thrill of militia days and the fine horses of the New Rumley Guards and because West Point was the nation's top military school. The academy also stressed other skills, such as management and engineering, which were becoming important in the nation's expanding economy. West Point graduates who didn't go on to become soldiers often became successful lawyers, bankers, and railroad and business executives.

Autie faced several obstacles. For one thing, West Point was a demanding school. Many young men either failed the entrance exam or would later drop out under the academic pressure. Autie was bright, but he was not a disciplined student. In addition, entrance to the

To acknowledge that he accepted his appointment to the U.S. Military Academy at West Point, George Armstrong Custer signed and returned this January 29, 1857, form letter from the U.S. secretary of war. The letter was also signed by Autie's father, Emanuel Custer, who gave his parental consent for his son's appointment and service as a cadet.

academy was tied to national and local politics, and U.S. congressmen controlled appointments for cadets, as students at the academy were called. The Custers, thanks to Emanuel's strident opinions, were known to be fervent Democrats. The Ohio congressman who controlled the appointment process, John A. Bingham, was a Republican. Even more daunting, 1856 was an

This engraving, *West Point Military Academy: Cadets at Drill on Plain*, was published in an 1862 book by Benson J. Lossing called *Cadet Life at West Point by An Officer of The United States Army with a Descriptive Sketch of West Point*.

election year. Bingham was under tremendous pressure from his supporters to give the West Point cadetship to the son of a Republican.

Despite these obstacles, Autie got the coveted appointment. Exactly how it happened remains a mystery, but there is some evidence that two other local Republicans convinced Bingham to give young Autie the cadetship. One of these men was the father of a girl who was in love with Autie, a romance of which the father did not approve. Supposedly, he recommended Custer for West Point to keep him away from his daughter. Autie also passed the entrance exam. He could bear down and concentrate when he was forced to.

Autie became so fond of the academy that he would later call it his favorite place. West Point provided the military companionship he had so craved as a boy at militia day. The academy also set boundaries that he needed to control his behavior. Discipline was strictly enforced. A cadet could be punished for all sorts of things, from shabby dress to not standing at attention.

Failure to obey the rules resulted in a cadet receiving a demerit, or a "skin" as students called them. If a cadet accumulated 200 skins in a year, he could be expelled. Most cadets didn't want to get any skins if they could help it. The prankster Autie looked at it somewhat differently. To his way of thinking, the limit set by West Point authorities was 199 skins. He could have

Custer, shown in 1857 holding a picture of his girlfriend, Mary Holland, often expressed himself best in letters. He wrote this poem for her: "Dear Mary, thy eyes may prove less blue, Thy Beauty fade tomorrow, But Oh, my heart can ne'er forget Thy parting look of sorrow."

as much fun as he wanted, so long as his grades were adequate and he didn't earn 200 demerits.

Autie's record of pranks and jokes at West Point was far more impressive than were his grades. He tied tin pans to the tail of a professor's dog. He cooked and ate another cadet's pet rooster. One day in Spanish class, Autie asked the teacher how to say "class dismissed" in Spanish. When the teacher answered, the class walked out. "He is too clever for his own good," said Tully McCrea, one of his roommates. "He is always connected with all the mischief that is going on and never studies any more than he can possibly help." In one year, he collected 151 demerits. In another year, he earned 192. Yet he stayed within the boundaries and never reached the limit of 200.

What Autie valued most were the lasting friendships fostered by West Point's military setting. "He was beyond a doubt the most popular man in his class," another cadet wrote. His friends called him Fanny, partly because of his curly yellow hair, partly because of his fair, girlish skin tone, and partly because Autie's innocence appealed to them. Some of his best friends at the academy also had nicknames, such as Thomas Rosser of Texas, who was called Tex.

It is some measure of Custer's personality that many of these friendships were never broken, even though they were formed during the most divisive period in American history. By the late 1850s, the United States was being torn apart. Northerners and southerners had been arguing for a long time over a number of complex issues. The most important dispute concerned slavery. Many northerners were beginning to oppose slavery and didn't want to see it spread into the far West. Many southerners wanted slavery to expand into the new territories. They saw black slaves as property and argued that the U.S. Constitution protected their property rights. Although a large number of southerners realized that slavery would not be profitable in the West, they worried that if slavery was restricted, northerners would abolish it where it already existed.

Cadets at West Point couldn't help but be caught up in the controversy. Both northerners, such as Custer, and southerners,

The debate over slavery heightened in the United States after the passage of the 1854 Kansas-Nebraska Act. This act allowed settlers in the territories of Kansas and Nebraska to decide by popular vote whether these regions would permit slavery within their borders. After the act was passed, both pro- and antislavery activists flooded the two territories with their supporters, hoping to sway the vote. In Kansas outbreaks of violence over the act were so frequent that the region became known as Bleeding Kansas. Violence also spread to Congress and the Senate. Many delegates began arming themselves with guns when they went to work.

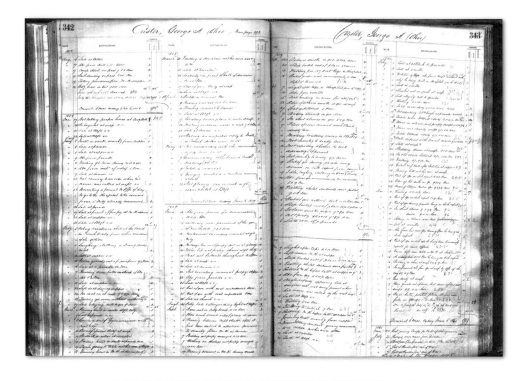

These logbook pages contain the Register of Delinquencies for Cadet George A. Custer. The entries detail the demerits that Custer accumulated between August 1858 and July 1860. Custer's numerous violations of West Point's rules and regulations included being late for both dinner and inspection, arriving at inspection without his bayonet, making an improper reply to an instructor, laughing and talking in class, and visiting a division that was not his own.

such as Rosser, attended the academy. If the dispute resulted in war, each side would rely on West Point cadets to form the backbone of its army. Custer wrote in a letter to his stepsister, Ann, that talk of war was on everyone's lips. The excitement was such, he said, that "I have scarcely thought of anything else."

In November 1860, Abraham Lincoln was elected president. For many southerners, Lincoln's election was a terrible blow. He was a Republican, and Republicans had pledged to confine slavery and allow it to remain only where it already existed. Seven southern states, led by South Carolina, left the Union between December 1860 and March 1861. These states formed the Confederate States of America, and elected Jefferson Davis as their president. In response to the secession of the southern states, Lincoln announced that his priority as president was to restore the Union.

The outbreak of war appeared to be just a matter of time. Many southern cadets left the academy to fight for their states. The cadets who remained faced January examinations. Autie, already a poor student, could scarcely concentrate with all the excitement and failed. The instructors understood that these were not normal times and decided to give him and thirty-two other failed students a second chance. If Autie did not pass, he would be expelled. Panicked because he was still not prepared to retake his exams, Autie broke into a professor's office and copied the exam questions. The professor discovered the break-in and created a different exam.

Custer passed, much to his own surprise, enabling him to remain at the academy. Many of his southern friends, though, were leaving, and it was becoming apparent that he would have to face them, as enemies, on the battlefield.

4. Autie Custer's First War

George Armstrong Custer was still at West Point when the Civil War began. On April 12, 1861, Confederates opened fire on Fort Sumter, a fort in the harbor at Charleston, South Carolina, which was occupied by U.S. troops. Two days later, the U.S. troops surrendered. When Lincoln called for a volunteer army of seventy-five thousand men to crush the Confederate rebellion, four more states left the Union and joined the new Southern nation.

Once, Custer's problem had been how to get into West Point. Now his problem became how to get out. West Point cadets normally were required to complete five years of instruction, which meant that Custer's class was not due to graduate until 1862. Because the country needed trained soldiers desperately, the academy crammed one year of classes into a special six-week session. Bleary-eyed and exhausted, Custer graduated along with thirty-three other cadets in late June 1861. Custer was, however, ranked dead last in his class.

While waiting for his army assignment, Custer remained in camp at West Point. On June 29, he was

The Bombardment of Fort Sumter, Charleston Harbor: 12th & 13th of April, 1861, a lithograph, was created by the firm of Currier & Ives around 1861. Nathaniel Currier and James Merritt Ives were business partners who specialized in mass-produced art that documented famous events in nineteenth-century America. Over a period of fifty years, which included a change to creating images with more pleasant subjects, the firm produced more than seven thousand prints.

appointed officer of the day, which meant that he was in charge of the camp. A scuffle started between two cadets. Custer was supposed to break up the fight. Instead he encouraged it. "Stand back boys," he said to a crowd of onlookers, "let's have a fair fight." For not doing his duty, Custer was brought before a court-martial, a trial held before military officers. In peaceful times, when officers didn't have more urgent issues to consider, Custer might have been severely penalized. He might even have been

kicked out of the army. Instead, Custer received only a letter reprimanding his conduct.

Meanwhile, Confederate and Union armies were gathering in Virginia. Ever since May, when the Confederacy had moved its capital from Montgomery, Alabama, to Richmond, Virginia, the state had become especially important. The state's proximity to Washington, D.C., only heightened the possibility that it would become a battleground. The Confederates were camped at Manassas, Virginia, about 35 miles (56.3 km) southwest of Washington. The Union army was coming together in Washington and was preparing to attack.

Custer finally received his assignment and left West Point on July 18, 1861. He was posted to the Second U.S. Cavalry as a second lieutenant. The regiment was already on its way to fight at Manassas. In just four days, Custer had to leave West Point, stop in Washington to collect important military orders, find a horse, and then report to the army.

On the morning of July 21, the Union army attacked the Confederate army in what became known as the First Battle of Bull Run. In the afternoon, a powerful Confederate counterattack pushed the Union army off the battlefield. The inexperienced

Opposite: Cadet George Armstrong Custer was photographed around 1859 in his West Point uniform. He is holding a Colt Root pocket revolver.

Union soldiers panicked and retreated in a frenzy. The Confederates gloried in the outcome. For Lincoln and the Union, the battle and especially the retreat were embarrassing.

Custer and the Second Cavalry did not see heavy action in the battle. While other combat units charged the enemy or defended against aggressive Confederate attacks, the Second Cavalry guarded supplies and mostly stayed behind the main battle lines. The war did not get more exciting for Custer for some time.

In October, while the Union army was still camped around Washington, D.C., Custer fell ill. Exactly what he had is unknown, but disease was common in the army. Disease, in fact, killed more soldiers on both sides during the Civil War than enemy bullets did. Fatigue might have worsened Custer's condition. He obtained a leave from the army and returned home. Custer was away from the army for five months. He spent part of that time with his parents in New Rumley, Ohio, and part at his stepsister Ann's house in Monroe, Michigan.

During his leave, Custer recovered from his sickness, but he also proved that he had yet to grow up. There was a darker side to Autie Custer's love of fun. Along with his pleasure in playing jokes on others,

Previous spread: The First Battle of Bull Run was depicted in a lithograph by Kurz & Allison around 1889. When the frightened Union soldiers made their hasty retreat from the battlefield, they left their guns, cannons, and flags behind.

Custer enjoyed gambling, drinking alcohol, and flirting with women. One night in Monroe, he got so drunk that he stumbled through the streets, yelling and laughing. Many of Ann's neighbors saw and heard him. The neighbors were angry at the disturbance, and Ann was deeply embarrassed. When Custer reached Ann's house, she made him promise that he would never drink again. He kept the promise to the end of his life. Unfortunately, some of Ann's neighbors, particularly a local judge named Daniel S. Bacon, would remain angry and suspicious of him.

Custer returned to the army in February 1862. Much had changed. The Union army, led by George B. McClellan, was more disciplined, better equipped, and stronger than it had been at Bull Run. In March, McClellan and his one hundred thousand men boarded ships, sailed from the outskirts of Washington to Fort Monroe in Virginia, and began marching on Richmond, Virginia, from the east.

General George B. McClellan was photographed by Mathew Brady around 1861.

Custer distinguished himself during the march with his leadership, his bravery, and his uncanny ability to find out what the enemy was doing. Custer soon caught McClellan's attention. Partly to reward him, but primarily because he needed daring, courageous men at his side,

McClellan appointed Custer to his personal staff. At age twenty-two, Custer became an aide to the army's commanding general.

Unfortunately, the appointment had a drawback. If McClellan failed, then those people closest to him were also tainted with failure. In late June and early July, the Confederates, led by Robert E. Lee, counterattacked and drove McClellan away from Richmond. Two months later, Lee invaded Maryland. Although McClellan forced Lee to retreat after the Battle of Antietam on September 17, McClellan moved and fought too cautiously. The Union army won the battle, but Lincoln thought that McClellan could have destroyed Lee's army and maybe even have ended the war. Frustrated with McClellan, whom he accused of having a bad case of the "slows," Lincoln removed him from command. Because Custer had served on McClellan's personal staff, he too was removed. Custer returned to Monroe.

In life, then as now, many people do not get a second chance. McClellan never again commanded an army or fought in the war. Custer was more resilient. He would soon be back in the war, serving under other, more aggressive generals.

Custer got a second chance in his personal life, too. Back in Monroe, he began to court Elizabeth Bacon, the daughter of the judge who had been so upset at Custer's drunken antics the previous winter. Daniel Bacon didn't want Libbie, as Elizabeth was called, to have anything to

In spite of losing her mother and three siblings at an early age, Elizabeth Bacon Custer, shown here in 1862, was an optimist. She graduated valedictorian, or first in her class, from Boyd Seminary in 1862.

do with the young soldier. Libbie herself wasn't sure if she wanted to have anything to do with him either. Custer was as persistent in love as he was in war. Libbie remarked that one day Custer walked by her house more than forty times.

Libbie eventually agreed to exchange letters with Custer, as long as they wrote to each other in secret. Slowly she found herself falling in love. Whether Judge Bacon would ever approve of Custer was another matter.

5. Wolverine in Blue

While George Armstrong Custer was at home courting Libbie Bacon, the war had begun to change from fighting that was cautious and controlled to battles that were fiercer and more destructive. Lincoln had also changed the Union's war goals. In 1861 and during most of 1862, he wanted only to preserve the nation. After the Battle of Antietam, Lincoln's goals expanded to include abolishing slavery. Shortly after the battle, Lincoln announced the Emancipation Proclamation, which went into effect on January 1, 1863. The proclamation freed slaves in rebellious Southern states. Lincoln could not enforce it, however, unless the North won the war. Because both sides had more to fight for, the South to keep slavery and the North to abolish it, both sides fought harder.

Custer returned to the war in May 1863. He reported to a camp in Virginia, where the armies had recently fought at Chancellorsville. The battle had been a Confederate victory. Soon after, the Confederates began to march north toward Pennsylvania. As this Confederate campaign to invade the north began, Custer was assigned

Edwin Forbes created this 1863 pencil drawing depicting a cavalry charge near Aldie, Virginia, where the Union cavalry led by General Alfred Pleasonton engaged the Confederate cavalry commanded by J.E.B. Stuart. At the outset of the war, the South had the advantage of having more soldiers who had grown up in the country riding horses.

to the staff of Alfred Pleasonton, who commanded the cavalry of the Army of the Potomac. Custer was given the rank of captain.

The same leadership qualities that were apparent to McClellan were apparent to Pleasonton. As the Confederate army moved northward through Virginia and into Maryland, the cavalries of the two armies engaged in several bloody skirmishes. The Confederate cavalry fought fiercely because it didn't want the Union cavalry to advance and discover where the main Confederate army was located. The Union cavalry was equally fierce because it was precisely this information the Union generals sought.

Custer seemed to be everywhere during these skirmishes, scouting, fighting, and leading men in combat. Although his low rank put him below many of the actual commanders of these skirmishes and didn't entitle him to give orders, Custer seemed to take control during key moments in the fighting. "If Lt. Custer observed that it was important to make a movement or charge," wrote a witness to many of these incidents, "he would tell the commander to do it, and the commander would have to do it, would not dare question, because he knew Lt. Custer was working under Genl. Pleasonton who would confirm every one of his instructions and movements."

Custer's assignment to Pleasonton turned out to be his career's most critical turning point. Pleasonton was determined to reform the army's cavalry. Previously, the Union cavalry guarded supplies, spied on the enemy, and protected the main army as it marched. Pleasonton wanted to turn the cavalry into a mobile, aggressive attacking force. He also wanted men like Custer, men who were young, fearless, and open to new ideas, to command the troopers in battle.

In late June, as the Confederates entered Pennsylvania, Pleasonton asked the Union army's new commander, George Gordon Meade, to promote Custer and two other staff officers to the rank of brigadier general. Meade agreed. Most promotions came one step at a time, but Custer leaped four grades from captain to general. He was just twenty-three, the youngest general in the Union army. One reason that Custer fought so boldly was to attract attention to himself. Custer was ambitious and eager to be promoted to a higher rank. Still, he could

This Civil War–era surgical kit belonged to Dr. Charles C. Lee, an assistant surgeon who tended the 1st Maryland Volunteer Cavalry and was later assigned to the U.S. Army as a contract surgeon. A major advance in wartime medicine was the systemized use of ambulances and stretcher bearers, who were trained to take the wounded quickly from the battlefield. This 1862 innovation was the idea of Jonathan Letterman, the medical director of the Army of the Potomac.

hardly believe that he now led a brigade. "To say I was elated," Custer wrote in July 1863, "would faintly express my feelings."

A brigade consisted of several regiments. Custer's brigade, the Michigan Cavalry Brigade, contained about 2,300 men and was made up entirely of soldiers from Michigan. The men became fiercely loyal to Custer, who took great pains to inspire them. His general's uniform, for example, was dazzling. He wore a suit of black velvet, trimmed with luxurious gold lace. His spurs and buttons glittered, his shined boots glistened, and his crimson tie seemed aflame. Most generals preferred the standard and less flashy uniform specified in regulations. Custer chose to dress flamboyantly to make himself stand out. Although the enemy could more easily spot him as a target, he reasoned that his own men could also see that he was in the thick of the fight with them. Custer's men willingly followed him into battle because they knew he would not take them where he would not go himself.

In early July, the opposing armies met at Gettysburg, Pennsylvania, and fiercely fought for three days. On the third and last day of the battle, while the infantry dueled to a climactic finish, the cavalry forces fought their own separate battle behind the Union lines.

Opposite page: This 1863 portrait of Brigadier General George Armstrong Custer shows him outfitted in his self-fashioned velvet uniform, including gold braid on his jacket and two stars sewn onto the collar of his shirt.

At two critical moments, Custer personally led desperate charges. "Come on, you Wolverines!" he shouted to his men. The second charge was particularly dramatic. Custer waved his sword defiantly as his men plowed into the Confederates. "So sudden and violent was the collision," wrote one eyewitness, "that many of the horses were turned end over end and crushed their riders beneath them." This charge drove the Confederates from the field. Custer's rallying cry became a lasting nickname for his men.

Gettysburg forged a strong bond between General Custer and his men. The Union cavalry had never beaten the Confederate cavalry before. Custer's men knew they followed a commander who could win. A similar change was occurring throughout the infantry, for Meade had achieved an important victory at Gettysburg. The Union army had turned the tide of the war.

At Gettysburg, Custer became a national hero. Word of his incredible promotion had already reached his family in New Rumley. The news had also reached Monroe, where Custer was still trying to win the hand of Libbie Bacon. Custer's bravery at Gettysburg seemed to confirm that he deserved to be a general. The people in Monroe who had once been suspicious of him began to respect him, particularly as he was leading Michigan boys into battle.

One Monroe citizen who changed his mind about Custer was Daniel Bacon, Libbie's father. On February 9,

The Custers were photographed by Mathew Brady's studio around 1865. On her wedding day, Libbie wore a pale green dress and a brooch that held a lock of her mother's hair. Daniel Bacon, Libbie's father, worried that the couple's wedding gifts might be stolen while they were on their honeymoon so he moved the gifts to the bank for safekeeping.

Philip Sheridan's ride from Winchester to Cedar Creek, Virginia, to rally his troops, dramatized here in a chromolithograph by Thure de Thulstrup from around 1886, was the subject of a poem by Thomas Buchanan Read. "The heart of the steed and the heart of the master/ Were beating like prisoners assaulting their walls,/ Impatient to be where the battle-field calls . . . Hurrah! hurrah for horse and man!"

1864, with both bride and groom dressed impeccably, Autie and Libbie were married in a Monroe church.

With Libbie accompanying him, Custer reported to Virginia for what would prove to be the climactic year of the war. Despite the victory at Gettysburg, Lincoln was still dissatisfied with the slow progress of his armies and had turned to yet another general to save the Union. This general, Ulysses S. Grant, was the man who would ultimately succeed. Grant replaced Alfred Pleasonton with Philip H. Sheridan, a fiery commander whom Grant trusted. Within months, Custer and Sheridan would themselves become close, and their partnership outlasted the war.

In May, Sheridan won an important victory over Confederate troopers at Yellow Tavern, Virginia. Then in August, while the main Union army laid siege to Petersburg, Virginia, Grant ordered Sheridan to take command of another Union army in Virginia's Shenandoah Valley. The Shenandoah Valley, which was west of Richmond and the main fighting, had always been a difficult region for Union generals. The Confederates grew much of their food supplies there and the valley was like a highway that led straight to Washington, D.C. Confederates had often marched through it to threaten the Northern capital. Sheridan's job was to clear the Confederates out of the valley permanently.

Sheridan and Custer were well suited for this campaign. First at Winchester, and then at the Battle of Fisher's Hill, Sheridan defeated the Confederates and pushed them southward. Then Sheridan's forces set barns, crops, and even some homes on fire. The Burning, as Shenandoah Valley residents came to call it, was an example of the Union's harder war.

Sheridan burned the crops to keep food from Confederate troops and to propel a faster victory. On October 19 at Cedar Creek, the Confederates attacked in a desperate attempt to stop Sheridan. General Sheridan, who was about 12 miles (19.3 km) away at the start of the

Thomas Rosser, above, and Custer resumed their friendship after the war. In 1873, the men enjoyed spending time together when Rosser became chief engineer of surveyors for the Northern Pacific Railroad.

During the fighting in the Shenandoah Valley, Custer confronted the Confederate cavalry of his old West Point friend Thomas Rosser. Although the men were still friends, Rosser was also the enemy and Custer wanted to beat him.

On October 9, the cavalries squared off at the Battle of Toms Brook. Custer paraded out in front of his men and, in grand style, saluted his Southern friend. Within moments, though, Custer attacked and drove Rosser's cavalry from the town of Woodstock in such a panic that the battle became known as the Woodstock Races. Custer even captured one of Rosser's uniform coats.

Always the prankster, Custer wore the coat in camp although it was far too big for him. He also sent a note to his old friend, asking Rosser to have a tailor shorten his other coats.

Alfred Waud created this October 7, 1864, eyewitness drawing of the burning of Virginia's Shenandoah Valley near Mount Jackson. Custer and the cavalry are depicted in the foreground. As these rough sketches were made into engravings, Waud noted details that might be added later. In the upper right area of the sketch he scribbled, "Custer carried a riding whip."

battle, rode furiously to the scene and rallied his troops to an incredible victory.

The Burning scorched the valley so thoroughly that it was never used again by Confederate generals. Custer performed so brilliantly during the campaign that he was given command of a division.

6. A Warrior Without a War

By April 1865, Philip Sheridan, George Armstrong Custer, and the cavalry had rejoined General Grant's army near Petersburg, Virginia. On April 2, Grant launched a massive attack at Petersburg. The Confederates retreated from Petersburg and began racing westward, hoping to outrun Grant's pursuing army. Like a pack of hunting dogs, Custer and the Union cavalry nipped at the Confederate army until it was worn down near a village called Appomattox. On April 9, a Confederate officer rode toward the Union troops bearing a white flag.

After four hard years of war, Custer was the lucky officer to receive the enemy's flag of surrender. Later that day, Grant met the Confederate commander, Robert E. Lee, in a nearby house, where Lee formally surrendered his army.

When the meeting ended, Philip Sheridan bought the table where Grant had been sitting. He gave it to Libbie Custer. "Permit me to say, Madam," Sheridan wrote to her, "that there is scarcely an individual in our service

Alfred Waud sketched this April 9, 1865, drawing of a Confederate officer approaching Brigadier General George Armstrong Custer at Appomattox with a flag of truce. The flag (*inset*) had once been part of a white linen dishtowel.

Key to Painting

From left to right, to the cabinet: Lt. Col. Charles Marshall, Lt. Col. Ely S. Parker, Gen. Robert E. Lee, Lt. Col. Orville E. Babcock, Lt. Gen. Ulysses S. Grant, Maj. Gen. Edward O. C. Ord, Lt. Col. Horace Porter, Capt. Robert T. Lincoln, Lt. Col. Theodore S. Bowers

Starting from the cabinet, clockwise: Maj. Gen. Phillip H. Sheridan (leaning forward), Brig. Gen. Rufus Ingalls, Lt. Col. Adam Badeau, Brig. Gen. George H. Sharpe, Brig. Gen. Michael Morgan, Brig. Gen. Seth Williams, Brig. Gen. John Rawlins (*back view*)

Keith Rocco's 2001 painting *Surrender at Appomattox* depicts Generals Grant and Lee shaking hands after successfully negotiating the terms of peace. The officers gathered in the parlor of Wilmer McLean's home in the village of Appomattox Court House. The Appomattox Court House National Historical Park commissioned this work as other paintings have depicted the historic surrender incorrectly. This depiction, however, was based on eyewitness accounts.

who has contributed more to [our victory] than your very gallant husband."

On May 23 in the nation's capital, Custer and the rest of the Union army grandly paraded down Pennsylvania Avenue and past the White House. The applause from the crowd was thunderous. Custer, always the showman, galloped past the main grandstand, his golden hair and flaming red tie flowing in the wind.

War had brought out the best in Custer, yet there was no longer a war. Army duty in peacetime was often hard, lonely, and boring. If Custer chose to remain in the army, he faced an added problem. In the Civil War, he had commanded volunteer soldiers. His rank was based on that command. He was, in other words, a major general of U.S. volunteers. If Custer stayed in the regular army, his rank would fall to captain. A lower rank would limit his authority and restrict his control. A captain of cavalry, for example, commanded only about 60 men.

Although he toyed with the idea of starting another career, Custer eventually chose to stay in the army. He was assigned to duty in Louisiana and Texas. Custer's supposed mission in the summer of 1865 was to put down any lingering Confederate resistance in Texas. His real purpose, however, was to assemble a cavalry unit in Louisiana and then move the troopers to Texas to provide a show of force. Napoléon III, the emperor of France, had sent his army into Mexico with the hope of creating a French empire there. The United

Mathew Brady took this May 1865 photo of the Grand Review of the army down Pennsylvania Avenue in Washington, D.C. Over a two-day period, 150,000 men paraded before President Andrew Johnson, General Ulysses S. Grant, and thousands of spectators.

States did not want France to think it could invade America, too.

Custer soon ran into problems. The men he commanded that summer were not the same men he had commanded in the war. The men had volunteered to fight in the Civil War. The war was over and the men wanted to go home. As there was almost no combat, Custer could not prove himself to this new command. Rather than trust and obey Custer, the soldiers rebelled against him and constantly broke his rules. Custer resorted to harsh disciplinary measures. He whipped some men and shaved their heads. He executed at least one soldier for desertion.

The only goodwill that Custer received came from his family. Libbie joined him on the mission, as did his brother Tom, who had also fought in the Civil War. In addition, Custer used his influence to have his father, Emanuel Custer, hired as an agent in charge of obtaining supplies for the cavalry.

Thomas "Tom" Custer, photographed by D. F. Barry around 1870, received two Congressional medals of honor for his bravery during the Civil War.

Early in 1866, while the cavalry was stationed in Austin, Texas, the mission ended. However, that was not the end of Custer's misery. Some Republicans in the North, sometimes called Radicals, wanted to treat the South harshly for their rebellion. Many of these Radicals also wanted to make sure that the emancipated slaves were protected and that black men were allowed to vote. Other northerners, including many Democrats, wanted to be lenient toward the South, and many did not want black men to vote. Unfortunately, these northerners did not think blacks were equal to whites. Custer was among the Democrats who called for mercy and opposed giving voting rights to black men.

Custer's opinions were similar to the opinions of Andrew Johnson, who became president when Lincoln was assassinated in 1865. Johnson wanted to treat the South leniently and had been a southern Democrat from Tennessee before the war. Johnson had opposed secession and had aligned himself with the Republican Party during the war. In 1866, many Republicans, who opposed his light treatment of the South, accused Johnson of betraying the North and the Republicans. Hoping to use Custer's fame to his advantage, Johnson asked Custer to join him on a speaking tour of the North. The trip, which was called the "swing around the circle," was a disaster. Johnson heaped abuse on his audiences and his political opponents. At several stops, he even traded insults with hecklers. Custer's popularity suffered from his

Andrew Johnson was the first president in U.S. history to be impeached. Members of Congress, angered that Johnson had fired Secretary of War Edward Stanton without obtaining Senate approval, voted to have Johnson removed from office. A vote to convict Johnson of wrongdoing did not pass in the Senate and he remained in office.

association with the president. Johnson was so unpopular that Congress eventually tried to remove him from office.

In July, Congress reorganized the regular army. Custer was offered the rank of lieutenant colonel in a new regiment, the Seventh Cavalry. Because it was regular duty, the rank was actually a significant promotion from his previous regular-army rank of captain. Custer was not a general anymore, but everyone continued to call him General Custer in recognition of his rank and achievement during the Civil War. If everything went just right in his postwar career, Custer might be made a general for good.

7. Frustrated Frontiersman

Understanding the people who are heroes in American history can sometimes mean learning some sad, uncomfortable truths about them. George Armstrong Custer is no exception. Both before and after the Civil War, Custer and most white Americans believed that anyone who wasn't white was inferior. White people thought that only they were intelligent and capable of progress. They saw people of other colors, such as blacks and Indians, as stupid and lazy. They thought blacks and Indians were savages who would delay white progress.

In some ways, Custer benefited from this hateful prejudice. After the war, the regular U.S. Army had two main objectives. The first was to occupy the defeated South. The second was to fight and control the Indian nations on the western frontier. In time, public opinion would turn against the troops in the South. The soldiers stationed there were seen as forcing white southerners to do things against their will. They were also viewed as treating black people better than white people. Because Custer did not serve long in the South after the war, he avoided

A Lakota Sioux village near Pine Ridge, South Dakota, was photographed by John C. H. Grabill around 1891. In the foreground, the Sioux's horses are drinking at the White Clay Creek watering hole.

the perception that he was favoring blacks at the expense of whites. At the same time, because he would soon fight against Indians on the frontier, he was perceived as helping whites.

Custer joined his new regiment, the Seventh Cavalry, in October 1866. The regiment was stationed at Fort Riley, Kansas. The cavalry was assigned a number of tasks. The soldiers were to protect settlers on the Santa Fe and Smoky Hill Trails, the main roads from central Kansas to Santa Fe, New Mexico, and Denver, Colorado.

Crew members of the Northern Pacific Railroad were photographed around 1885. Workers laid tracks over the most isolated territory in the United States. Traditionally, railroad crews worked six days per week from dawn until dusk.

The primary spur to white settlement in the West was the railroad. Between the Civil War and the turn of the century, railroad companies built thousands of miles of track. The railroads made western lands easy to get to. They carried crops, minerals, and goods to markets, and they employed thousands of people.

Railroad companies also acted as land agents. The state and federal governments gave companies almost 180 million acres (72.8 million ha) of public land. The companies often sold the land to settlers and used the profits to pay for laying tracks. As a result, whole towns sprung up along railroad tracks. The railroads were important for other, more emotional reasons as well. They were symbols of white progress and American patriotism. The railroad routes that linked the East Coast to the West Coast were called transcontinental railroads. The first transcontinental railroad, completed in 1869, tied the nation together.

The cavalry was also to protect the Union Pacific Railroad, which was still being constructed. Most important, the cavalry was to keep peace with the western Indian tribes and to keep the frontier safe for white settlers.

These were not easy tasks. After the Civil War, a massive tide of settlers began to stream westward. Almost four million people came in just twenty years. Many were farmers, cattle herders, and merchants. Other large numbers of settlers included miners and day laborers who were looking to strike it rich on gold. These settlers often came to established western states, such as Kansas, Nebraska, Nevada, California, and Oregon. They also pushed into frontiers such as Colorado, New Mexico, Wyoming, and the Dakotas, which were still territories.

This wave of settlers crowded against the people who were already there. About 270,000 Native Americans made their homes west of the Mississippi River. Although many white Americans lumped the Indians together as one group, the Indians were actually members of at least 125 different tribal groups. Some of these groups got along with one another while others warred. Some, such as the Cherokee in Oklahoma, were recent arrivals. The U.S. government had forced the Cherokee to move there from Georgia and other southern states in the 1830s. The Nez Percé, and the Apache, however, had been in the West for centuries.

Before the Civil War, many Americans thought the West was a vast, barren land that they did not wish to settle. The government even tried to make a permanent boundary for what was called Indian country, or the land west of the great bend in the Missouri River.

In 1851, the government signed treaties with many of the tribes after a meeting at Fort Laramie, Wyoming. These treaties separated the Indian nations from one another and confined them to specific areas of land called reservations. White settlers often ignored the treaties, and federal agents often cheated the groups out of the goods and supplies that had been promised to them by the government. After the war, as more white settlers flooded the frontier, many people began to see the West as a paradise, and not an empty land.

William Henry Jackson photographed Fort Laramie in 1868. Available housing at army forts was based solely on rank. The size of an officer's family was not taken into account. Many soldiers and their wives, Custer and Libbie included, occasionally lived in tents.

This painting of a Lakota Sioux camp was done by Karl Bodmer. The Lakota Sioux were made up of groups such as the Oglala, the Miniconjou, the Sihasapa, the Hunkpapa, the Sans Arc, the Brulé, and the Two Kettle.

The government estimated that about one hundred thousand of the Indians were hostile to white settlers. Many of these hostile Indians were called Plains Indians because they roamed the plains of Kansas, Nebraska, Wyoming, Colorado, and the Dakotas. The most powerful of the Plains nations, such as the Sioux, the Cheyenne, and the Arapaho, were fierce warriors. These nations resented white settlers because whites made it harder for them to hunt buffalo. The buffalo provided almost everything that Indians needed to survive. A buffalo's meat was nutritious, the hide was fashioned into clothing and shelter, and even the tendons were used for making bow strings. Millions of buffalo roamed the West, sometimes in such vast herds that miles (km) of land looked black to a person viewing them at a distance. White settlement was destroying the buffalo at an alarming rate. By 1900, in fact, the animal was almost extinct.

The beginning of Custer's frontier life was not promising. The men in the Seventh Cavalry were not the best troops. The soldiers were lonely, bored, and many drank alcohol to pass the time. A number of the men joined the regiment because they had nothing better to do and would soon desert. Although many had fought in the Civil War, none of the men, not even Custer, had any experience fighting Indians. Even when the regiment was trained into a good fighting force, a number of the men and officers came to hate Custer, for Custer often punished them in the same way that he had punished the men in Texas.

On December 21, 1866, a band of Sioux Indians under Chief Red Cloud wiped out an entire party of white soldiers in an ambush near Fort Phil Kearny in Wyoming. Although Wyoming was far from Kansas, white leaders feared that Red Cloud's attack would provoke Indian attacks elsewhere. In March 1867, General Winfield S. Hancock ordered a march against the Cheyenne and Sioux Indians in Kansas. Custer led the cavalry. Although Hancock intended to talk to the

Chief Red Cloud, leader of the Oglala Sioux, was quoted in an 1871 U.S. Commissioner of Indian Affairs report: "The Great Spirit raised both the white man and the Indian. I think he raised the Indian first. He raised me in this land and it belongs to me. . . . I have given [the white man] room. There are now white people all about me. I have but a small spot of land left. The Great Spirit told me to keep it."

This view of Fort Hays, Kansas, was taken in 1873. Along with protecting the railroad construction workers and the settlers in the region, Fort Hays served as a supply depot. Goods that were transported via the nearby Union Pacific Railway were unloaded and stored at Fort Hays. Later, these supplies were transported to other forts south and west of Fort Hays.

groups, the Indians fled. Custer pursued, but he was unable to find them. After burning an empty Indian village, Custer led his men to Fort Hays, Kansas, where he remained until May.

During his stay at Fort Hays, Custer became lonely and depressed. He was far away from Libbie, who was still at Fort Riley. The frontier seemed like a strange, distant place, especially when compared to the battlefields of the Civil War. Custer must have sensed that his men either didn't like him or didn't like army life; ninety men deserted in just six weeks.

In June and July, Custer and his men marched into Nebraska and Colorado, where travelers and settlers had complained of Indian attacks. He was directed to keep the area between the Platte and Republican Rivers clear of Indians. Custer was so lonely and determined to see Libbie again that his mind was fogged. Some men died because Custer started making bad decisions. Other soldiers were worn to exhaustion, along with their horses, when Custer strangely ordered the men to march into an area that he wasn't directed to explore. By July, when the men reached Fort Wallace, Kansas, they were dispirited and broken down. Several more soldiers deserted.

When he reached Fort Wallace, Custer was set on seeing Libbie at Fort Riley. He took some of his men and forced them to march 150 miles (241.4 km) to Fort Harker, where Custer could board a train to Fort Riley and pick up his wife. The men marched without a break, and some soldiers fell behind and were attacked by Indians. Finally, though, Custer reached Fort Riley and Libbie.

Libbie and Autie were together, but only at the cost of some of his men's lives and their faith in Custer's ability to command. Many men never forgave Custer for putting his personal interest above their safety and welfare. Custer was court-martialed for placing his men in such danger. This offense was more serious than his court-martial at West Point, six years earlier, and so was the penalty. Custer was suspended from the cavalry for a year. Considering that his decisions had cost some of his men their lives, the punishment could have been much worse.

8. A Life on the Plains

George Armstrong Custer's actions in 1867 showed how devoted he was to his wife, Libbie. She was equally devoted to him. Some people said that their marriage was like a fairy tale. That wasn't quite true. Frontier life was hard, lonely, and uncertain. The Custers argued, as do many married couples. Still, it is almost impossible to picture one without the other. During Autie's court-martial, Libbie wrote that the Custers were "determined not to live apart again."

Custer desperately needed to feel loved, to believe that others could depend on him. Libbie filled this need, especially in 1867, when it was obvious that his men didn't like him. Tom Custer, who was a lieutenant in the Seventh Cavalry, made Custer feel like a protective older brother. Custer also took comfort in dogs. He had become an avid hunter while stationed in Texas, and it was not unusual for him to have a pack of hounds trailing his every move. Once he even kept a pet pelican.

While Autie was suspended from duty, the Custers spent part of the time at Fort Leavenworth, Kansas, and

Autie and Libbie, along with their friends and family, were photographed in 1876 as they picnicked along the Little Heart River in the
Dakota Territory. Custer is at the center of the photograph in a white
jacket. His wife, Libby, is seated to his left.

the rest at home in Monroe, Michigan. Meanwhile,
much was changing on the Plains. The federal government had decided on another new policy with the
Plains Indian nations. In 1867 and 1868, the Indians
were talked into signing treaties that confined some of
the nations, including the Comanche and the
Cheyenne, to reservations in Indian Territory, or what
became present-day Oklahoma. Others, such as the
Sioux, were to stay on reservations in the Dakotas. By
moving the tribes south of Kansas and north of

The is a signature page from the Fort Laramie Treaty of 1868. Both U.S. Army officers and Native American leaders signed the document. This treaty specified that the Black Hills of the Dakota territory were part of the Great Sioux reservation.

Nebraska, the government hoped to clear the central Plains for white travel and settlement.

The new treaties, like the old ones, were unfair. Whites cheated Native Americans and stole supplies, such as blankets, food, guns, and leather goods, which were meant for the Indians. They also ignored the treaties by traveling on Indian land whenever they wanted. Many of the Indians also weren't aware that when they signed these treaties they were giving up their hunting lands in Kansas and Nebraska forever. Whites deliberately didn't tell them. The Indians "have no idea [what] they are giving up," a white witness to a treaty ceremony wrote in his diary. "The treaty all amounts to nothing, and we will certainly have another war sooner or later."

War broke out again in Kansas during the summer of 1868. The new commander in Kansas was Philip Sheridan, the officer who had furthered Custer's career during the Civil War. Sheridan used his influence to have Custer restored to service with the Seventh Cavalry. Sheridan was determined, as were other generals, to fight the Indians more aggressively. After serving about ten months of his suspension, Custer returned to duty in October 1868. Custer was eager to get started and immediately rejoined the Seventh, which was camped near Fort Dodge, Kansas.

Ordinarily, the threat of bad weather in the autumn months would have delayed any fighting until the following spring. However, because the tribes were more likely to stay in one area for long periods of time during colder weather, Sheridan realized that the Indians were more vulnerable in the fall and the winter.

In November, with Sheridan along for part of the trip, the Seventh Cavalry moved into Indian Territory, or present-day Oklahoma. Marching in a blustering snowstorm, the cavalry discovered the village of Black Kettle, who was the chief of a band of Cheyenne Indians. Although Black Kettle wanted peace with the whites, some of his young warriors had assaulted settlers in Kansas. At dawn on November 27, 1868, near the Washita River, Custer attacked the village. Black Kettle's people were surprised and confused and didn't stand a chance against the invaders. The battle, which lasted only ten minutes, devastated the village. Custer's men set huge bonfires, destroying clothing, food, and supplies. They also killed the village's entire herd of ponies, almost 900 in all.

Historians do not know how many Indians were killed in the battle. Custer estimated that 103 Indians were killed. What is known is that some women and children, whose lives were normally spared during combat, were slain. Also slain was Black Kettle himself, who was shot along with his wife as they tried to cross the river. Historians also know that the battle was intended as a message to Indians. If they did not peacefully move to reservations, they would be wiped out.

The Battle of the Washita began Custer's shift from a Civil War hero to a western hero. As he had been a symbol of the North's triumph over the South, he became a symbol of white conquest of the West. Yet he had made some serious mistakes. Custer had not bothered to scout the surrounding area of the fight. Had he done so, he would have discovered that he was outnumbered. Almost six thousand Indians were camped near the Washita River. Black Kettle had simply set up his camp, which included no more than 350 people, apart from the others. Custer's failure to detect this cost twenty of his men their lives. These twenty men had split apart from the rest of Custer's command and had unknowingly moved in the direction of the larger Indian camp. They were discovered, surrounded, and killed.

Charles Schreyvogel's 1904 painting *Attack at Dawn* depicts the Battle of the Washita. On the morning of the attack, heavy fog and a layer of snow masked the approach of the cavalry. As the soldiers came closer, the Cheyenne could hear a bugle. Custer frequently ordered his military band to play a rhythmic Irish tune called "Garyowen" when the cavalry marched or charged toward the enemy.

Custer always believed that once he had led men in combat they would follow him anywhere. That was not true after the Battle of the Washita. Fighting gave the Seventh Cavalry experience, but it did not tie the regiment to Custer. Many of the soldiers could not forgive Custer's decision to leave the battlefield before finding out what had happened to the missing men. Captain Frederick Benteen insulted Custer in a newspaper

Frederick Benteen, photographed by D. F. Barry around 1874, was respected by his men, for his "quiet steady" leadership.

article, accusing Custer of being more interested in shooting ponies for sport after the battle than in finding his missing soldiers. "Ah!" Benteen wrote sarcastically. "He is a clever marksman." The two men already disliked one another and almost fought with guns and horsewhips over the article.

Custer tried to follow his victory at Washita with other expeditions in the winter of 1869, but the weather was so bad that some of his missions were delayed. Custer did manage to have a meeting with a Cheyenne chief called Medicine Arrows. Medicine Arrows and a Cheyenne holy man smoked a peace pipe with Custer. According to several accounts, when they finished, the holy man tapped the ashes of the pipe onto Custer's boot and told him in Cheyenne that Custer and all of his men would be killed if Custer ever betrayed the promise of peace with the Indians. Custer didn't understand the meaning of the smoking ceremony. He did not understand the Cheyenne language or make any effort to learn it.

For the next few years, the cavalry did little fighting. Part of the regiment went with Custer when he was assigned to duty near Louisville, Kentucky, from 1871 until 1873. Even in Kentucky both Custer and the regiment remained firmly associated with the Plains. Once, for example, the son of the Russian czar, or king, visited him. Custer took leave of his duty in Kentucky and guided the czar's son, Grand Duke Alexis Romanov, on a buffalo hunt in Kansas and Colorado. Several newspapers printed stories about the trip, which increased Custer's national reputation.

During his stay in Kentucky, Custer discovered a hidden talent. A magazine asked him for stories about his experiences on the frontier. When Custer obliged, he

Custer and Grand Duke Alexis Romanov of Russia posed for this photograph before they embarked on their 1872 buffalo hunt. This hunt was more extravagant than most. The Duke's tent was carpeted and champagne was served each time he killed a buffalo. William "Buffalo Bill" Cody was hired as the scout for the expedition. He tracked the buffalo and brought the party to the site where the buffalo could be found.

found that he truly enjoyed writing. Writing was an outlet for his creative energies and "opened to him a world of interest," Libbie observed. His articles, which appeared in such popular magazines as *Galaxy* and *Turf, Field and Farm*, told of his western adventures against Indians and his hunting expeditions for buffalo. Many of his articles were put together in a successful 1874 book called *My Life on the Plains*.

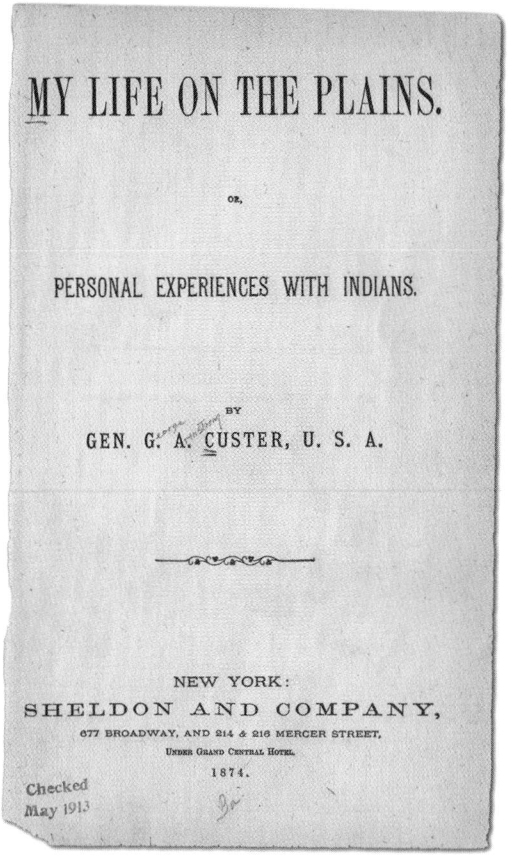

Thanks in part to his writing, Custer became the country's best-known frontiersman. In his early thirties he still had the golden hair, the boyish charm, and the freshness of a young man. As a frontiersman, Custer wore fur hats, leather boots, and buckskin shirts and pants fringed with tassels. Buckskin clothing was made from animal hide and was favored by many Indians and pioneers. These clothes

MY LIFE ON THE PLAINS.

OR,

PERSONAL EXPERIENCES WITH INDIANS,

BY

GEN. G. A. CUSTER, U. S. A.

NEW YORK:

SHELDON AND COMPANY,

677 BROADWAY, AND 214 & 216 MERCER STREET,

UNDER GRAND CENTRAL HOTEL.

1874.

Checked
May 1913

After reading Custer's 1874 *My Life on the Plains*, General William Tecumseh Sherman praised it as an excellent account of the Indian wars. Custer wrote at a table in his library. Although he preferred to be alone when he studied or wrote, Custer allowed a pet mouse to roam his desk and papers while he jotted down his thoughts. Shown here is the title page.

were just as important to his western image as his colorful uniform had been to his image during the Civil War.

Some evidence suggests that Custer was insecure or uncomfortable in his role as a frontier hero. His adventures in *My Life on the Plains* and his other writings were occasionally exaggerated for effect. To some of his soldiers, it appeared that Custer was glorifying himself and putting them down. Benteen was one of Custer's critics and unkindly called the book "My Lie on the Plains." There were also times when Custer wanted to leave the West. In 1869, he tried to get the job as commandant of cadets at West Point, but was turned down. In 1871, just before he went to Kentucky, Custer visited New York City to see if he might become a businessman. After considering the prospects, he chose to remain with the cavalry. Custer had once said that he "experienced a home feeling" with the cavalry "that I cannot find in civil life."

Not everyone in the regiment disliked Custer. Many of his men loved him. Autie and Libbie surrounded themselves with their friends in the regiment and often threw lavish parties. Custer treated these favorite soldiers and their wives especially well, so well that others sarcastically called his favorites "the royal family." As Custer did not treat everyone equally, it became another source of friction in the regiment. Granting favors was also another way that Custer had of making himself feel needed, wanted, and loved. He and Libbie were childless, and the couple came to think of the regiment as their frontier family.

9. To the Little Bighorn and Beyond

The great legend and legacy of George Armstrong Custer remains because of his last day on Earth. To many people, Custer's death at the Battle of the Little Bighorn was just as romantic and dashing as his life.

More ignored and broken treaties would shape the events that led to the Little Bighorn. This time the victims of white cheating were the Sioux, who lived in the Dakota Territory. Under a treaty signed at Fort Laramie in 1868, the Sioux were promised all the land in present-day South Dakota that is west of the Missouri River. Members of the Sioux nation were also allowed to hunt in large stretches of Montana and Wyoming. Most of the Sioux agreed to the treaty. The Sioux who opposed the treaty followed important leaders such as Sitting Bull, Gall, and Crazy Horse. They roamed the hunting lands and refused to report to the Dakota reservation. Because these Sioux rejected the treaty, whites feared them.

Two important developments added to the tension. The Northern Pacific Railroad wanted to lay tracks across the land promised to the Sioux. To protect railroad

Young-Man-Afraid-of-His-Horses, an Oglala chief, was photographed smoking a ceremonial pipe at Fort Laramie, Wyoming, during an 1868 treaty negotiation between the Lakota Nation and the United States. Pipes, filled with tobacco, were smoked to signify that a treaty or an alliance had been made with another tribe or the U.S. government.

employees, the federal government ordered the Seventh Cavalry to report to Fort Abraham Lincoln, usually called Fort Lincoln, near present-day Bismarck, North Dakota, in 1873. That same summer, Custer and his men led an expedition into the Yellowstone River valley, where engineers for the Northern Pacific were scouting for the best route for the new railroad. Several times the cavalry clashed with Sioux warriors.

The second development involved gold. Decades earlier, thousands of pioneers had streamed into California

This photograph from the 1870s shows George Armstrong Custer, his Native American scouts, and an unidentified man examining a map of Sioux country. Custer was in Montana Territory, instructed to protect the surveyors and builders of the Northern Pacific Railroad. On the tent are the initials N.P.R.R., which stands for Northern Pacific Railroad.

when gold had been discovered there in 1848. Whites had long believed that the precious metal could also be found in the Black Hills in southwest Dakota.

The area of the Black Hills was already promised to the Sioux, however. The Sioux believed that the Black Hills were sacred and holy, a serene place where they could experience powerful, spiritual visions. To take the Black Hills from them, the Sioux thought, would be to take away their souls.

In 1874, Custer and the Seventh Cavalry marched from Fort Lincoln to the Black Hills. Officially, the government said their mission was to look for a place to build a new fort. In addition, Custer's job was to see whether rumors of gold in the hills were true. What the expedition first found was "a rich and beautiful country," as Custer wrote to Libbie at Fort Lincoln, a landscape of stunning peaks and valleys, lush green grass and wildflowers, blue streams, and an astonishing array of wildlife. "It was as if the Almighty had set this place aside," one trooper wrote, "and put a sign on it that read: 'No white men wanted here!'"

Miners with the cavalry expedition also found a small amount of gold. Once the discovery of gold was made known, whites demanded that they be allowed to enter the Black Hills and that the Sioux be kept out.

In late 1875, President Ulysses S. Grant, who benefited from his Civil War fame and was elected U.S. president, made two key decisions. First, he said, he would not

This 1874 photograph of the Castle Creek valley in the Black Hills of South Dakota, taken by Illingworth, documented the passage of the Black Hills expedition wagon train. The 110 wagons that made up the train usually traveled in four columns. General Custer and his scouts protected the train in the front, the cavalry guarded the wagons on the sides of the columns, and a group of infantry kept watch behind the train. The wagon train was aligned into a single file, however, when it went through narrow terrain such as this area of the Castle Creek valley.

enforce the 1868 treaty keeping whites out of the Black Hills. Almost immediately, settlers by the thousands poured into the Hills on what the Sioux began calling the Thieves' Road. Grant's second decision ordered all the Sioux to go to the Dakota reservation. No longer could the bands of warriors under Sitting Bull, Crazy Horse, and the other chiefs who had rejected the treaty roam the hunting grounds in Montana and Wyoming. Should they fail to report to the Dakota reservation, the army would bring them in.

The year 1875 was one of the happiest years that Custer and Libbie spent together. The couple shared a spacious house in Fort Lincoln, where Custer continued to recount his western adventures in essays for newspapers and magazines. The next spring this interlude came to an end. The Sioux bands in the hunting grounds had refused to report to the Dakota reservation. Just as the Seventh Cavalry was preparing for war, Custer was suddenly called to Washington to testify before Congress.

Many Democrats in Congress wanted to keep Grant, a Republican, from winning a third term as president. They said his administration was full of corruption, and they aimed many of their attacks at William Belknap, the secretary of war. One of Belknap's duties was to oversee the practices of private businessmen at U.S. Army forts on the frontier. Belknap's enemies accused him of accepting bribes. In one case, Belknap had agreed to let a group of private businessmen set up a store at Fort Sill, Oklahoma. In exchange for having the only store at the fort, which protected them from competition and allowed them to charge high prices for goods, the businessmen were said to have paid Belknap and other influential people about $12,000 per year. The Fort Sill case was one of several such shady deals at army forts. Grant's own brother, Orvil, was involved in some of them.

Custer, still attached to the Democratic Party politics of his father, testified against Belknap and Orvil Grant in Congress. His testimony confirmed that his instincts for politics were not as sharp as his instincts for war. Custer did not testify out of a sense of duty. He did so primarily to help the Democrats.

President Grant was furious. He felt betrayed and almost didn't let Custer lead the cavalry in the upcoming campaign against the Sioux. Only the pleading of Custer's friends, particularly Generals Philip Sheridan and Alfred Terry, changed Grant's mind.

The Army's plan for tracking and capturing the Sioux in the Wyoming and Montana hunting grounds had three parts. One group of men, led by General John Gibbon, was to march eastward from Fort Ellis, Montana. Another group of soldiers, under General George Crook, was to move north from Fort Fetterman in Wyoming. The last group, under General Terry, was ordered to move west from Fort Lincoln, Dakota. Because no one knew exactly where the Sioux were

From left to right: Shown are portraits of Tom Custer, Boston Custer, and Harry Armstrong Reed. Before the cavalry left Fort Lincoln, Custer quickly wrote a letter to Libbie, "Do not be anxious about me . . . I hope to have a good report to send you by the next mail."

located, the first task was to find them. Then, once the Indians were spotted, the different groups would converge and catch the Indians between them.

Custer, working under General Terry, led the Seventh Cavalry. This was a special and happy trip for Custer, for in addition to his brother Tom, his youngest brother Boston and his nephew Harry Armstrong "Autie" Reed were to accompany him. Boston, or Bos, and Autie Reed wanted to see the West.

The men left Fort Lincoln on May 17. For the first

few weeks, they sighted no Indians. As the march continued, scouts began to find evidence of recent Sioux camps. On June 21, General Terry came up with a plan. He guessed that the Indians would be camped near the Little Bighorn River. Custer and his regiment were ordered to follow Rosebud Creek and then turn toward the Little Bighorn. Meanwhile, Terry would join up with Gibbon's men and move around to the north. If Custer found the Indians near the Little Bighorn, he would attack the Sioux and drive them northward, right into the arms of Gibbon and Terry's men.

Custer and the Seventh Cavalry, about six hundred men in all, moved out on June 22, 1876. The march along Rosebud Creek took three days and proved to be hot, dusty, and tiring. Finally, on June 25, Custer's scouts spotted the Sioux camped in a valley near the Little Bighorn. What the scouts saw alarmed them. The Sioux village was huge. Exactly how large it was is still not known, but no one in the cavalry expected so many Indians to be assembled in one place. The bands of Crazy Horse, Sitting Bull, Gall, and other Sioux war chiefs were gathered there. Additionally, Native Americans who normally stayed on the Dakota reservation had also joined this assembly. As many as six thousand Indians from more than ten different nations, including the Cheyenne and the Arapaho, made up the village amassed in the valley. Anywhere from eight hundred to two thousand of these Indians were warriors, and they were in high spirits. On

June 17, they had defeated General Crook's soldiers at the Battle of the Rosebud.

Custer was not scared. He only feared that the villagers would discover him and flee. His goal was to attack the Sioux by surprise, as he had done at the Battle of the

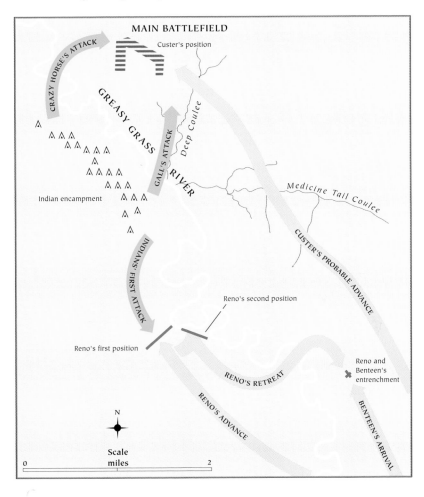

This map shows the relative position and movement of Custer's men led by Custer, Reno, and Benteen, as they moved toward the Native American encampments at about noon on June 25, 1876, before the Battle of the Little Bighorn.

Washita. Custer divided his men into four battalions. Frederick Benteen, in charge of one battalion, was sent to the south to make sure there were no Indians in that area. The other battalions moved toward the village. In midafternoon, Custer attacked. One of the battalions, under Major Marcus A. Reno, splashed across the Little Bighorn River and struck the lower end of the Sioux village. His attack caught the Sioux off guard. Many of the warriors had slept late, as they had stayed up most of the night celebrating their victory at Rosebud Creek. Meanwhile, Custer took the last two battalions, containing about 225 men, along the east side of the river. From this point onward, historians can only guess at Custer's intentions. He probably planned to strike the Sioux from the northern end of the village.

Historians do know that Custer saw the first stages of Reno's attack and wanted to make sure that the entire regiment had enough ammunition for a strong fight. As he watched Reno's men fighting across the river, Custer ordered that a message be taken to Benteen, whose battalion had the supplies. "Benteen," the message read, "Come on. Big Village. Be Quick. Bring Packs." Historians also know the outcome of the battle, because the Sioux left many accounts. However, there are gaps in what we know because no one who was with Custer that afternoon lived. All these years later, the mystery of Custer's final hour tempts us to imagine what transpired.

Reno's attack, which was meant to pin the Sioux down, fell apart as soon as the Indian warriors recovered from their surprise and fought back. Reno first retreated to a tree-lined area near the river. Panicked, he ordered his men back across the Little Bighorn. Many of his troopers were killed as they tried to escape. Although Reno was so rattled that he could no longer command, the remaining men made their way to a hilltop where they dug in and tried to hold off the advancing Sioux warriors. Benteen's men soon joined them. Despite Custer's order to "Be Quick," Benteen had marched slowly on his return to the regiment. Still,

Custer's last message to Benteen was written down by his adjutant, Lieutenant William Cooke, who handed the paper to the bugler, Giovanni Martini, for delivery.

Following spread: *Custer's Last Stand* was depicted by Edgar S. Paxson in 1899. Custer is shown in the center of the painting wearing buckskins and a red scarf, and holding two revolvers. The Battle of the Little Bighorn remained an exceedingly popular subject to paint for decades after the battle was waged.

The Native American artist Kicking Bear created this 1898 painting of the Battle of the Greasy Grass. Custer is seen to the left of center wearing yellow buckskins. At the lower right of the image, Sioux women organize a victory dance. Standing in the center of the image are (*left to right*) Sitting Bull, Rain-in-the-Face, Crazy Horse, and Kicking Bear.

Benteen's leadership on the hill steadied the men. For the rest of the day and most of the next, the soldiers on the hill kept the Indians at bay.

During this time, Custer remained east of the Little Bighorn. He was separated from the rest of his men, which had been part of his plan. Unfortunately, Reno's

retreat doomed Custer's strategy. Because Reno was backtracking, many warriors in the village turned to attack Custer. The warriors, led by Crazy Horse and Gall, poured over the river in enormous numbers and surrounded Custer's battalions. They wiped out Custer's soldiers, man by man.

The battleground was hilly and was situated about 5 miles (8 km) away from Benteen's hilltop. Because of the gullies and depressions in the ground, the Sioux could creep closer to Custer's men without being hit by the cavalry's bullets. As Benteen and his men were far away, the Indians could fight without worrying that another battalion would come to Custer's rescue.

No one knows when Custer died. Legend has it that he was one of the last to fall. His body was found on a ridge that was later called Custer Hill. He lay near Tom, Bos, and Autie Reed. Custer had started the day in his famous buckskin suit. He was found naked, a bullet hole in his left temple and another one in his left side. Whether a sewing awl had actually pierced his eardrums only the two Cheyenne women, who later described their actions to Kate Bighead, knew for sure.

10. Heroes and History

Two days later, on June 27, men from General Terry's group rode upon the scene of devastation. By that time, the Sioux had left their camp on the Little Bighorn and had retreated into the nearby mountains. Many of Frederick Benteen's surviving soldiers saw Terry's men from a distance and thought they might be George Armstrong Custer's lost battalions. They had not heard anything from Custer for two days.

General Terry's men were shocked by what they saw. "It was the most horrible sight my eyes rested on," said Lieutenant Francis Gibson. Not only had Custer's men been stripped of their clothing, but to celebrate their victory the Sioux had also scalped and mutilated many of the men's bodies. News of the disaster soon made its way eastward. From all corners of the country, newspapers called out for revenge. Back in Monroe, Michigan, the whole town mourned. At Fort Lincoln, a soldier knocked on Libbie's door and sadly told her that Autie was dead. She was heartbroken. "To lose him," she said later, "would be to close the windows of life that let in the sunshine."

She was not the only woman at Fort Lincoln who felt that way. Twenty-six soldiers who were also husbands had been killed.

People asked how Custer and his men could have been wiped out. Custer's critics, both then and now, blame him for the massacre. They say he should not have divided his men. Military commanders had been taught never to divide their forces when facing superior numbers. The critics also say Custer should never have attacked the Sioux village. The encampment was simply too big. Custer should have waited for Gibbon's and Terry's men to join him.

Some critics go even further and say Custer attacked because he wanted all the glory for himself and the Seventh Cavalry. They say, too, that Custer hoped to be elected president. The year 1876 was an election year, and, had Custer won the battle, he would have become even more popular than he already was.

The truth is more complex. Although conventional military rules said not to divide a command when outnumbered, Custer did not know exactly how many warriors he faced, nor did he care. His experience on the frontier had already shown him that the conventional way of doing things often did not work in the West. He knew that the Sioux, like many other Indians, were concerned foremost with protecting their families. Custer made the assumption that individual Sioux warriors would panic at a surprise attack and would rush to protect their families rather than fight back as a group.

It was not rash of him to attack immediately. Custer could have waited for help, but he thought that the Indians were alert to additional cavalry in the area. Had the Indians escaped, Custer's soldiers stood little chance of catching them. Custer's frontier experience had taught him this lesson as well.

Historians know from Sioux accounts that although the Indians were surprised, the Sioux did not panic. Some blame for the failed attack must also fall on Major Reno, who did not press his attack for long enough. In 1879, Reno was investigated by the military for his conduct at the battle. He was not punished, but only because the army preferred to avoid additional controversy. Blame must also fall on Benteen, who did not march his men as swiftly to the battlefield as he should have. Benteen's slow pace might have resulted from his hatred of Custer.

Clearly, Custer made mistakes. If he was going to take such a daring risk and divide his command, he should have had a tactical understanding of the hilly and broken ground that became the battlefield. Instead, he had not sent out his scouts, just as he had not scouted at the Battle of the Washita. Such risks should only have been taken with experienced officers and soldiers, who might have remained calmer when Custer's plan failed. Sioux accounts of the battle suggest that many of Custer's

These four Native Americans from the Crow nation had served as Custer's scouts. They were photographed by Joseph K. Dixon at the Little Bighorn battlefield in 1909, standing beside grave markers that honored the fallen soldiers of the Seventh Cavalry.

soldiers were too scared to fight well. Many troopers were new to the Seventh Cavalry, and many of the regiment's officers were absent from the regiment as they were assigned to other duty.

For his plan to have been carried out perfectly, Custer needed luck. On June 25, he didn't have it. There is a reason why the odds were stacked against him. The Sioux fought better than he did. They won. It is misleading to call the battle Custer's Last Stand. Instead, the battle was the greatest Native American victory over whites in the West.

After the battle, Custer and the rest of the dead men were buried on the battlefield. Some men of the Seventh Cavalry are still there. The next summer soldiers returned to the site, collected the remains of other soldiers, and sent them eastward for reburial. Custer was taken to West Point, for he had asked Libbie to make sure that he was buried there. "Its traditions," Libbie later wrote, "were dear to him."

Libbie Custer, photographed in 1910 in the garb of a widow, lost many members of her family at the Battle of the Little Bighorn.

Custer's many admirers wanted

CUSTER MONUMENT, MONROE, MICH.

Edward Potter's monument to George Armstrong Custer, *Sighting the Enemy*, was dedicated in Monroe, Michigan, on July 4, 1910. The monument depicts Custer astride his horse at the Battle of Gettysburg, in which he led the soldiers of the Michigan Brigade to victory against the Confederate forces of General J.E.B. Stuart.

to make sure that Custer was never forgotten.

Libbie was especially active in preserving his legacy. In later years, she wrote three successful books about her life with Autie. When she died in 1933, Libbie had been a widow for almost fifty-seven years. She was buried beside her husband at West Point.

Libbie's books strengthen the legend of Custer that arose in his lifetime. Monuments to his memory were built on the battlefield and at other places in the country. Later Americans would celebrate him by writing books, painting pictures of the Last Stand, and making movies about his life. It was said that the only cavalry survivor of Custer's Last Stand was Comanche, the horse of Captain Myles Keogh. When Comanche died around 1891, he was stuffed and put on display at the University of Kansas.

The Custer legend has helped to obscure what happened to the Sioux and the other Indian nations of the West. The Sioux won the battle, but the Little Bighorn was their final victory. Within a year, the Army had cleared the tribe's hunting lands. Crazy Horse surrendered to the government in 1877. He was later stabbed and killed by a soldier when he resisted being locked up in a guardhouse in Fort Robinson, Nebraska. Sitting Bull first fled with his band to Canada, then surrendered in 1881. He was shot and killed in 1890 by authorities who were worried about unrest on the Dakota reservation. The Army and the western Indians would continue to clash from time to time, including one terrible day at Wounded Knee, South Dakota, in 1890. Nonetheless, the American nation eventually extended from the Atlantic to the Pacific Ocean.

The Sioux, too, want to remember Little Bighorn. To them, the battle represents a triumph of their people. Their defense of their lands also exemplifies the pride and dignity of all Indian nations. In 1991, Native American activists and other supporters convinced Congress to change the name of the national park at the battlefield. The original name, Custer Battlefield National Monument, celebrated only Custer. The new name, Little Bighorn National Monument, acknowledges

This photo shows the monument to Crazy Horse, chief of the Oglala Sioux, which is being carved into the Black Hills of Custer, South Dakota. Construction on the memorial was begun by the sculptor Korczak Ziolkowski in 1948. The left arm of Crazy Horse is raised to answer a white man who asked, "Where are your lands now?" The warrior responded, "My lands are where my dead lie buried."

the Indians and their victory. The Indians are also building their own monuments, not just at Little Bighorn, but also in the Black Hills. For more than fifty years, a family of sculptors have been carving a statue of Crazy Horse into the Black Hills, only a few miles (km) from Mount Rushmore. Native Americans want us to know that their heroes, like the presidents on Rushmore, and like George Armstrong Custer, were also American heroes.

Timeline

1839   George Armstrong Custer is born in New Rumley, Ohio.

1846–48   The United States defeats Mexico in the Mexican War and acquires vast territory in the West, including California.

1851   The U.S. government and the leaders of some western Indian nations sign the Treaty of Fort Laramie.

1857   Autie Custer enters West Point in June.

1861   Southern states form the Confederate States of America.

The Civil War begins.

Custer graduates from West Point and joins the Union army.

1862   Custer is appointed to the staff of General George B. McClellan.

1863   Custer is promoted to brigadier general.

The battle of Gettysburg, a Union victory, turns the tide of the war.

1864   Custer marries Elizabeth "Libbie" Bacon.

Philip H. Sheridan and Custer defeat Confederate forces in the Shenandoah Valley of Virginia.

1865   The Civil War ends.

Custer goes on duty in Louisiana and Texas.

1866   Custer is appointed lieutenant colonel in the new Seventh Cavalry.

Custer joins President Johnson on his "swing around the circle" tour.

1867   The Seventh Cavalry begins to fight Indian nations in Kansas and Nebraska.

The U.S. government signs the Medicine Lodge Treaty with western Indian nations.

Custer is court-martialed and is suspended from duty.

1868   Custer returns to duty and wins the Battle of the Washita in Oklahoma.

1869   The Union Pacific railroad, the eastern leg of the first transcontinental railroad, is completed.

1871   Custer reports for duty near Louisville, Kentucky.

1873   Custer leads the Yellowstone expedition.

1874   Custer's book, *My Life on the Plains*, is published.

Custer leads soldiers into the Black Hills, where miners accompanying him discover gold.

1876   Custer testifies before Congress.

Custer dies at the Battle of the Little Bighorn.

1933   Libbie Custer dies.

Glossary

allure (uh-LUR) The power of attraction.

Apache (uh-PA-chee) A Native American nation that lived in the American West.

Arapaho (uh-RA-puh-hoh) A Native American nation that lived in the American West.

awl (OL) A sharp, pointed tool used to punch holes in leather or wood.

bleary-eyed (BLEER-ee EYD) When a person's eyes are droopy and watery from exhaustion.

cavalry (KA-vul-ree) The part of an army that rides and fights on horseback.

charisma (kuh-RIZ-muh) Charm or magnetism.

Cheyenne (shy-AN) A Native American nation that lived on the western plains.

Comanche (kuh-MAN-chee) A Native American nation that lived on the western plains.

compelling (kum-PEH-ling) Demanding attention.

Constitution (kon-stih-TOO-shun) The basic rules by which the United States is governed.

distinguished (dih-STING-wishd) Something that stands out and is marked as superior or different.

divisive (dih-VY-siv) Causing argument or dissent.

Emancipation Proclamation (ih-man-sih-PAY-shun prah-kluh-MAY-shun) A paper, signed by Abraham Lincoln during the Civil War, that freed all slaves held in Southern territory.

encampment (en-KAMP-ment) The place where a group of troops has set up a camp or a campsite.

expelled (ek-SPELD) To be removed from a place.

fervent (FUR-vint) Impassioned, to be filled with strong emotion or passion.

inexpressible (ih-nik-SPREH-suh-bul) Hard to put into words.

interlude (IN-ter-lood) A length of time that separates one time period or event from another.

lenient (LEE-nee-unt) Of mild or tolerant disposition.

lurid (LUR-id) Shocking.

militia (muh-LIH-shuh) A group of volunteer or citizen soldiers who are organized to assemble in emergencies.

Nez Percé (NEZ PURS) A Native American nation that lived in the American West.

outskirts (OWT-skerts) A place far from the center.

pellets (PEH-lutz) Small, round objects, often fired from a weapon.

plains (PLAYNZ) An area of mostly flat lands that have few or no trees.

prejudice (PREH-juh-dis) Disliking a group of people different from you.

rambunctious (ram-BUNK-shis) Very active and rowdy.

resilient (rih-ZIL-ee-int) Strong, capable of withstanding pressure or blows without suffering any lasting damage.

ruthlessness (ROOTH-les-nes) To show no compassion or mercy toward another.

Sioux (SOO) A Native American people from North America's plains.

troopers (TROO-perz) Soldiers who were enlisted in the cavalry.

uncanny (un-KA-nee) Mysterious; almost supernatural.

Additional Resources

Books

Brennan, Kristine. *Crazy Horse*. Philadelphia, PA: Chelsea House
Publishers, 2002.

Burks, Brian. *Soldier Boy*. San Diego: Harcourt Brace, 1997.

Clinton, Catherine. *Scholastic Encyclopedia of the Civil War*. New York:
Scholastic Reference, 1999.

Kalman, Bobbie. *Nations of the Plains*. St. Catherines, Ontario: Crabtree
Publishing Company, 2001.

Web Sites

Due to the changing nature of Internet links, PowerPlus Books has developed an online list of Web sites related to the subject of this book. This site is updated regularly. Please use this link to access this list:

www.powerkidslinks.com/lalt/gacuster/

Bibliography

Barnett, Louise K. *Touched by Fire: The Life, Death, and Mythic Afterlife of George Armstrong Custer*. New York: Henry Holt, 1996.

Brinkley, Alan. *American History: A Survey*. New York: McGraw-Hill, 1991.

Brown, Dee Alexander. *Bury My Heart at Wounded Knee: An Indian History of the American West*. New York: Henry Holt, 2001.

Connell, Evan S. *Son of the Morning Star: Custer and the Little Bighorn*. San Francisco: North Point Press, 1984.

Frost, Lawrence A. *The Custer Album: A Pictorial Biography of General George A. Custer*. Seattle, WA: Superior Publishing Company, 1964.

Michno, Gregory F. *Lakota Noon: The Indian Narrative of Custer's Defeat*. Missoula, MT: Mountain Press Publishing, 1997.

Monaghan, Jay. *Custer: The Life of General George Armstrong Custer*. Boston: Little, Brown, 1959.

Moulton, Candy Vyvey. *Everyday Life Among the American Indians*. Cincinnati: Writer's Digest Books, 2001.

Neihardt, John G. *Black Elk Speaks*. New York: MJF Books, 1996.

Nevin, David. *The Soldiers*. New York: Time-Life Books, 1973.

Utley, Robert M. *Custer: Cavalier in Buckskin*. Norman, OK: University of Oklahoma Press, 2001.

Wert, Jeffry D. *Custer: The Controversial Life of George Armstrong Custer*. New York: Simon & Schuster, 1996.

White, Richard. *"It's Your Misfortune and None of My Own": A History of the American West*. Norman, OK: University of Oklahoma Press, 1991.

Index

About the Author

Paul Christopher Anderson is an assistant professor of history at Clemson University, where he has taught since 2000. He is the author of *Robert E. Lee: Legendary Commander of the Confederacy*, another book in the Library of American Lives and Times series, as well as *Blood Image: Turner Ashby in the Civil War and the Southern Mind*, published by Louisiana State University Press. He and his wife, Keri, live in South Carolina with their two dogs, Mandy and Gracie.

Primary Sources

Cover. *Major General George Armstrong Custer*, photo, ca. 1864, Mathew Brady, Bettmann/CORBIS, background, *Custer's Last Fight*, lithograph, ca. 1895, Otto Becker, Milwaukee Lithographic Company. **Page 4**. *George A. Custer in a Major General's Uniform*, silver gelatin print, ca. 1864, Mathew Brady's Studio, Still Picture Branch, National Archives and Records Administration (NARA). **Page 6–7**. Seventh Cavalry near Fort Hays, photo, 1869, Kansas State Historical Society. **Page 10**. *Bismarck Tribune*, newspaper clipping, July 6, 1876, South Dakota State Historical Society/ State Archives. **Page 13**. Custer's birthplace, photo, Ohio State Historical Society. **Page 14**. *Emanuel Custer*, photo, Monroe County Historical Museum; *Maria Custer*, photo, Monroe County Historical Museum. **Page 19**. U.S. Military Academy application letter, January 29, 1857, NARA, Old Military and Civil Records. **Page 20**. *West Point Military Academy: Cadets at Drill on Plain*, engraving, 1862, West Point Museum Collection, U.S. Military Academy Archives. **Page 21**. George Armstrong Custer holding a daguerreotype of a young belle, hand-colored copy print of a daguerreotype, 1857, the Granger Collection. **Page 24**. Custer's demerits, U.S. Military Academy. **Page 27**. *The Bombardment of Fort Sumter, Charleston Harbor: 12th & 13th of April, 1861*, hand-colored lithograph, Currier & Ives, 1861, Library of Congress Prints and Photographs Division. **Page 28**. Cadet George Armstrong Custer in his West Point uniform, Ambrotype, ca. 1859, National Portrait Gallery, Smithsonian Institution. **Page 30–31**. *Battle of Bull Run—July 21st 1861*, lithograph, ca. 1889, Kurz & Allison, Library of Congress Prints and Photographs Division. **Page 33**. *General George. B. McClellan*, photographic print on carte de visite, ca. 1861, Mathew Brady, Library of Congress Prints and Photographs Division. **Page 35**. *Elizabeth Bacon*, 1862, Monroe County Historical Museum. **Page 37**. Cavalry fight near Aldie, Virginia, pencil drawing, Edwin Forbes, 1863, Library of Congress Prints and Photographs Division. **Page 39**. Surgical kit, Civil War era, manufactured by J. H. Gemrig, National Museum of American History, Smithsonian Institution. **Page 40**. George Armstrong Custer, Ambrotype, 1863, National Portrait Gallery, Smithsonian Institution. **Page 43**. *Gen. and Mrs. George A. Custer*, photo, ca. 1864, Mathew Brady's Studio, Still Picture Branch, NARA. **Page 44**. *Sheridan's Ride*, chromolithograph, ca. 1886, Thure de Thulstrup, L. Prang & Co., Library of Congress Prints and Photographs Division. **Page 45**. *Thomas Rosser*, photographic print, Library of Congress Prints and Photographs Division. **Page 47**. The 3rd Custer div. on the 7th of Octr. retiring and burning the forage Etc. Somewhere near Mt. Jackson, drawing, 1864, Alfred R. Waud, Library of Congress Prints and Photographs Division. **Page 49.** Custer receiving the flag of truce—Appomatox [sic]—1865, drawing, 1865, Alfred R. Waud, Library of Congress Prints and Photographs Division. **Page 49.** Flag of truce, white linen dish towel, National Museum of American History, Smithsonian Institution. **Page 52.** Grand review of the Army, photo, 1865, Mathew Brady, Library of Congress Prints and Photographs Division. **Pages 53**. *Captain Tom Custer*, photo, ca. 1870, D. F. Barry, Western History/Genealogy Department, Denver Public Library. **Page 57.** Lakota Sioux camp on River Brule, photo, 1890, John C. H. Grabill, Picture History. **Page 58.** Northern Pacific Railroad Crew, including a Chinese man, photo, ca. 1885, Hulton Getty/Archive Photos. **Page 60.** Fort Laramie at the time of the Indian Peace Treaty of 1868, photo, 1868, William Henry Jackson, Harold B. Lee Library, Brigham Young University. **Page 61.** *Sioux Camp*, watercolor, Karl Bodmer, Joslyn Art Museum, Omaha, Nebraska. **Page 63.** *Red Cloud* (Maqpeya-luta), chief of the Oglala Sioux; photo, NARA. **Page 64.** View of Fort Hays, photo, 1873, Kansas State Historical Society. **Page 67.** Custer and Libbie, along with friends and family, photo, 1876, Hulton|Archive by Getty Images. **Page 68.** Fort Laramie Treaty of 1868, signature page, 1868, NARA. **Page 71.** *Attack at Dawn*, oil painting, ca. 1904, Charles Schreyvogel, Gilcrease Institute. **Page 72.** *Colonel Frederick Benteen*, photo, ca. 1874, D. F. Barry, Western History/Genealogy Department, Denver Public Library. **Page 73.** George Armstrong Custer and Grand Duke Alexis of Russia, photo, ca. 1872, Library of Congress. **Page 74.** *My Life on the Plains* (cover), 1874, published by Sheldon and Company. **Page 77.** *Young-Man-Afraid-of-His-Horses*, an Oglala chief smokes a ceremonial pipe at the 1868 treaty negotiations, photo, 1868, Smithsonian Institution, National Anthropological Archives. **Page 78.** *Lieutenant Colonel George Custer and Scouts*, photo, ca. 1870, Bettmann/CORBIS. **Page 80.** Expedition to the Black Hills, view of the Castle Creek Valley, photo, 1874, Illingworth, National Archives. **Page 83.** *Boston Custer*, *Harry Armstrong Reed*, photos, Monroe County Historical Museum, Captain Tom Custer, photo, ca. 1870, D. F. Barry, Western History/Genealogy department. Denver Public Library. **Page 87.** Custer's last message, paper, 1876, West Point Museum Collection, U.S. Military Academy. **Page 88–89.** *Custer's Last Stand*, oil on canvas, Edgar S. Paxson, Whitney Gallery of Western Art, Cody, Wyoming. **Page 90–91.** *The Battle of the Greasy Grass*, 1898, Kicking Bear, Southwest Museum. **Page 95.** *Four Crow Scouts*, photo, 1909, Joseph K. Dixon, Western History/Genealogy Department, Denver Public Library. **Page 96.** *Elizabeth Bacon Custer*, photo, 1910, Culver Pictures.

Credits

Photo Credits

Project Editor
Daryl Heller

Layout Design
Kim Sonsky

Series Design
Laura Murawski

Photo Researcher
Jeffrey Wendt